HERE THERE BE TYGERS

MICHAEL KUIACK

CLOCKWORK BOOKS

Here There Be Tygers

Copyright © 2017 by Michael Kuiack

All rights reserved. No part of this publication may be reproduced or used in any manner whatsoever without the express written permission of the publisher, except for the use of brief quotations in a book review.

Printed in the United States of America.

Clockwork Books
Kelowna, British Columbia, Canada

Cover image copyright tonefotografia/shutterstock.

Author photo by Mike Wood; used with permission.

First Printing, 2017

Print ISBN 978-0-9958654-0-2

Dedicated to
Bill Wilson and Bob Smith

A poem is never finished, only abandoned.
                          Paul Valery (1871–1945)

Contents

Miracle On South Street 1

When We Were Snowed In At Rehab 4

Two Chances With Anne D. 7

Bryan's Apartment... 9

When We Lived In Vancouver 10

Some Filipinos And A Hornet 12

Jealousy 14

Marilyn In Heaven 15

New Girl 18

Celina... 19

The Old House 22

Make Lots 25

Shame 26

I Am Martin Sheen 27

Hopeless... 29

Mascara.. 31

Grandpa 33

When We Are Apart 36

First Kiss... 37

Nancy... 42

Game Over.. 44

The Organ 46
He Has Lost Control Of The Angels 48
Here Is How It Is 49
Just Then, Just There 53
Hearsay 54
The Gap 61
Little Spoon 66
Blue In The Face 70
Life Is School 72

Miracle On South Street

In Room 611 – Pod A,
(NOTICE: This Room Under Video Surveillance For
 Your Safety)
There is a print of Monet's Poplars screwed tight to
 the wall.
There are 2 chairs roughly welded to iron
 stanchions.
There is a bed of sorts that does not move.
The air hisses cold from a ceiling vent.
The lights are controlled from elsewhere.
2 guards, barely teenagers, sit beyond the door,
(NOTICE: This Room Under Video Surveillance For
 Your Safety)
They laugh about golf and vacations and women.

If you lie on your right side,
On the bed of sorts that does not move,
In Room 611 – Pod A,
(NOTICE: This Room Under Video Surveillance For
 Your Safety)
If you look to the opposite wall,
There, near the Monet, almost to the corner,
You will see a blotch, a Rorschach splatter,
Where paint has peeled from cinder block,
Shaped like a misshapen M,
Block-ish, stylized, rotated to one side.

If you stare at the Rorschach splatter,
If you stare long enough,
If time is not an issue,
You will begin to see things in its rough edges,
Trimmed perhaps by finger nail,
Or water, or time.

You might see a gorilla face, all terrible fangs.
You might see an Easter Island head,
With worried, prominent brow,
Or two breasts with upright nipples,
One an A cup, one closer to a C,
A bear, rampant, with thick and dangerous shoulders,
A corner of Africa, the one near Khartoum,
Or there at the bottom right,
In perfect scale and detail,
In three-quarters profile,
Archie's sometime girlfriend, Betty,
Pretty, with her hair ribboned back.

If you stare at the wall of Room 611 - Pod A,
For even longer, harder,
If time is of no consequence,
If time hardly passes at all,
You might see it there,
Almost to the corner,
Scarcely bigger than the side of your thumb.
If you squint your eyes,

And drown out the screaming of the brown-
    skinned, bloody girl,
(NOTICE: This Room Under Video Surveillance For
    Your Safety)
Somewhere down the way,
Pining for her parents or angry or lost.
If you are able to quiet the klaxon in your brain,
And stop the trembles for a bit,
Concentrate and you will see,
A funny miracle,
Yogi's best friend, Boo Boo,
Kneeling, winged,
An angel in a pork pie hat.

When We Were Snowed In At Rehab

When we were snowed in at rehab,
I dreamed a Crown Royal dream.
I woke all angry, sweaty,
Jaw sore from clenching,
From crunching liquor-y ice,
Throat sore from the acrid bite,
Of marijuana smoke or screaming.

When we were snowed in at rehab,
The night shift left and was not replaced.
We were without Michelle,
Housewife and cook and dogs body.
She was trapped in Tiverton.
We made do with sandwiches and fried things,
Ice cream and peaches from a can,
Fruits and nuts and crackers.
Someone broke the microwave,
Heating a tin of soup.
The oven was beyond us,
It smelled of gas.

When we were snowed in at rehab,
Jimmy pumped tons of clanging iron.
It kept his mind off other things,
Off percs and his dead girlfriend, Polly.
He showered 6 or 8 times each day,
But always wore the same rank clothes.

When we were snowed in at rehab,
Cliff and Maggie played Rummy,
At one end of the dining room table.
Their game was eerie silent,
Just the occasional snick of a card,
A muttered 'cocksucker',
A whispered 'dirty whore'.
While one shuffled and dealt,
The other would stretch and look around.

When we were snowed in at rehab,
Fred walked a circuit of the first floor,
Stopping at this window or that.
The snow confounded Fred,
As if he did not remember the weather,
Or consider the change in seasons.
Things moved more quickly than Fred,
His every step was a journey,
Every breath was a carnival ride.

When we were snowed in at rehab,
Aaron painted pictures,
Of long dead prime ministers,
Painted all scary and dread,
Provincial governors of some erstwhile hell.
As he finished he pushed the portraits away.
They puddled on the floor.

When we were snowed in at rehab,

Sean acted all sullen and dour.
He huffed at the dead television,
He puffed at the floor.
He pretended to sleep the remainder of the day,
On the leather sofa in the lounge,
This was against all the rules.

When we were snowed in at rehab,
Julie tried to teach Jeff his manners,
With little success.
Jeff had come from the jungle,
He spat on the floor.
He knew only the civility of the crack house,
The courtesy of the pipe.
He claimed to have murdered a man.
No one called him on his shit.

When we were snowed in at rehab,
Brad drank tomato juice,
Mixed half and half with Drano.
He didn't die,
He puked a bubbling, blue-ish fluid,
He complained of cramps.
We tied him with strong, grey tape,
Around ankles, across scarred wrists.
We left him near the furnace,
Where he would be warm.

Two Chances With Anne D.

One time, the first time, in the front seat of a car,
In the driveway of Kim's parents' house in
   Woodstock,
On the long August weekend, the last summer of
   the 70's.
We spent the late of the night party there,
While the others slept in disarray.
We watched the moon over the top of the garage,
Talked about the stars, drinking sparkly blueberry
   wine.
I should have kissed you then.

You had been smoking,
I was drunk, of course,
I had taken some happy chemical.
In the morning I felt like 3 kinds of shit.

The second in your apartment on St. George,
On the floor in front of a ratty brown couch,
We were listening to Joe Jackson's *Steppin' Out*.
I had walked you home from the 'Wick,
Although I had no right,
You belonged to another in the titular sense.
Drunk again, drunk as a lord,
I kissed you then.
(Lips skinny as rakes, soft as kittens and strong.)
I got an attack of self-righteous,

And fled.

I remembered you today,
While I was trying to fill the hole.
I am afraid to Google you,
I am afraid you have Googled me.

Bryan's Apartment

My mind woke up in Bryan's attic apartment,
Kitchen, bedroom, bath,
Cain Street, opposite the Plaza Hotel.
Long, narrow, steep stairs,
The air never moved a muscle.

My body woke up at Bryan's dinette table,
Chipped and burnt and pitted Formica.
An ocean of bottles before me,
I drank without a glass.
Headband so I didn't drip on a drug.

I woke disturbed and fearful,
I could not return to sleep.
Troubled mind,
Matters must be addressed.

I run from sad and fond emotion,
I am impossible to love,
I am incapable of forgiveness,
Human touch makes my skin crawl.

Awake, I sat at the foot of the bed,
And considered the possibility,
That you had become,
A figment of my imagination.

When We Lived In Vancouver

When we lived in Vancouver,
She took the bus every morning,
To the top of the mountain.
She came home late and tired,
Lugging a pile of books.

When we lived in Vancouver,
I suspected she was fucking,
A fop named Paul,
Long hair tied back with leather,
An accent, vaguely British.
Didn't matter,
I was fucking a woman on the second floor,
Top of the stairs,
Overlooking the courtyard.
Her name was Michaela,
She never seemed to cum,
But she never said no.
She had big tits,
She shaved her snatch,
But had a thatch of hair under each arm.
We always did it on her living room floor,
To save the bed.

When we lived in Vancouver,
Our life was chaos.
Money tight, nerves raw,

Tempers explosive, futile.
Once she came at me with a paring knife,
High over her shoulder for a killing blow.
(I had made fun of a haircut,
Or a colleague, or a plan.)
I took the blade off the arm,
High, near the shoulder.
It left a jagged scar.
I raped her on the kitchen floor.
When I was finished,
She held me and kissed me soft and tender.
She whispered to me,
There on the kitchen floor,
In a pool of my blood,
Hard by the refrigerator.
Her stupid cat watched us from the hall,
Washing itself with spit wet paws.

Some Filipinos And A Hornet

In the coffee shop this morning,
I wanted to read the paper,
Have a coffee and a bite to eat.
The place was filled with Filipinos,
Dozens of Filipinos.
Old ones and baby ones and angry young men,
All speaking Spanish or whatever they speak.
They all spoke at once,
Or at least 8 at a time.
They all spoke loud,
Like they were ready to fight.
There was much laughter.

Thankfully, they were just packing to leave,
It became quiet after a while.
A woman came in with a boy,
Maybe 6 or 8 years old,
Old enough.
They bought some food,
They moved toward the tables, searching.
Suddenly the mother screamed,
A bona fide scream,
A late-night scream in a quiet neighbourhood.
A scream of rape, a scream of murder.
'Devon', she screamed,
'Get away from there right now'.
She was looking toward the window,

Looking like she was watching a car wreck,
Just about to happen.
She shook, the tray she was carrying went awry.
She was panicked,
She moved to corral the boy Devon,
Shield him with her arms.
The counter staff were catatonic, thunderstruck.
I looked to the window,
There was a hornet there doing hornet things,
Buzzing and banging the window,
All angry and stupid and proud.
I rolled up a section of my paper,
Strode to the window,
And smashed the hornet to death.
It left a smear on the glass,
Guts and hornet shit and blood.
I returned to my table and picked up my coffee for
    a sip.
She looked at me with a look that said,
You've wrecked him.
The boy looked at me with a look that said,
You've saved me.
I looked at them both with a look that said,
For fuck sakes, it was only a hornet.
I went back to my paper,
There was a garbage strike looming,
In some city somewhere,
It looked like there'd be hell to pay.

Jealousy

When I am making love with you,
In the house,
In the bedroom,
In the bed,
My jealousy is just outside the door.
My jealousy is doing press ups and chin ups,
It's doing the snatch, clean, and jerk.

When I am holding you to sleep,
Stroking your hair,
Whispering love words,
My jealousy is eating raw eggs,
It lies in wait.

Marilyn In Heaven

Once, after I had been in heaven a while,
A second or perhaps a lifetime or a year,
(Time is elastic in heaven,
Sticky and tricky and wide.)
I thought to seek out Marilyn.
She had a place facing the beach,
Beside and near-ish to me,
A mile or an ocean or a minute away.
(Space is foam rubber in heaven,
Sticky and tricky and wide.)
I came upon her lying on a deck chair.
Hi, said I.
Hi, said she.
Are you here to fuck me?
Or save me?
Or protect me?
Which one are you?
None of the above, I said.
I was just going to say hello,
Tell you I loved you in *The Seven Year Itch*,
But I can see you're busy right now,
Busy being a complete and haughty cunt,
So, I'll be on my way.
I turned to leave,
Things hadn't gone at all according to plan.
Wait, said she.
Do you want some juice to drink?

She seemed contrite and a little sad.
She was very, very pretty.
I said that would be fine.
I'm sorry about that she said.
She made a gesture with her chin,
As if her action was a presence around us,
As if it had left a smell.
It's tough for me in heaven, said she.
As tough as being alive.
It's men, she said,
I nodded and pretended to understand.
We drank red juice,
We sat the afternoon away until morning came to evening.
I told her how she had made me laugh in *The Seven Year Itch*,
How she made me horny,
How she made me squirm.
I told her how I had spent time in New York City,
When it was hot as hot could ever hope to be.
I told her I understood the heat and the crazy of the city,
That it made the movie better.
She told me about fucking Tom Ewell,
In his room at the Plaza Hotel,
How he raged when she didn't come,
How he slapped her face.
She told me stories about her crazy mother,
I told her stories about mine.
I asked her about Jack and Bobby,

Sure enough, it was true,
It was Bobby on the phone,
That night she took all the pills.
It was Jack who sent in the army,
To clean up all the mess.
We became friends,
After a while I came to love her,
Every man did.
Men caught Marilyn like a cold.

New Girl

"You're hairy," she whispers.
"I like hairy."
She combs persimmon fingers across my chest,
I watch a single hair fall to the carpet,
I feel ashamed,
I know the meaning of insubstantial.

"I love the smell of you," she whispers.
"You smell meaty, like a man."
She kisses my sternum for her lips are there,
I study the chestnut top of her head,
I breathe her.

We stand like that for the longest time,
Perhaps a day or a year.
She traces my nipples with ice cube fingers,
She kisses me softly here or there,
My arms hang limp at my sides,
I am paraplegic.

Behind her is a mirror,
Full-length on the wall.
Reflected, I see my anger,
I see the back of her,
Soft curves and deep shadows,
Skin and flesh and bone.
Lazarus-like, I reach for her there.

CELINA

Celina is pig-faced ugly,
Bulging eyes,
Prognathic jaw,
Sharp pointy nose,
Turkey wattles,
Eye brows and lashes,
Pale to invisible,
Fat body, small tits,
Thick ass, thick thighs,
Dank, stringy, horrid hair.

Celina is dumb as a post,
Unaware,
She talks too much,
Subjects of interest,
To her alone,
She likes to show off knowledge,
She doesn't have.

Celina lives with her mother,
Her father is long dead.
They complain about things together,
They watch reality TV,
They snipe at each other.
They are much alike.

When Celina is angry with Mother,

Which happens quite a lot,
She tries to kill herself.
She goes to the hospital.
Her Mother drinks,
Pretty much all of the time.

Celina dropped out of high school,
Because the children were so mean,
Celina was a sensitive child,
Her Mother said it was so.
She finished by correspondence,
Scraping by but just.

Celina dropped out of college,
Because the adults were so mean,
Celina was a sensitive adult,
Her Mother said it was so.

Celina has had two jobs,
Both ended badly.
Celina is a health nut,
Vegetarian, except for some meats,
Vegan, except for eggs.

Celina studies yoga,
Wants to be an instructor,
But she is too fat and slow and vacant.
The yoga school is stealing her money,
Five days a week.

Celina does not drive a car.
She has no passport.
She takes thirteen pills each day.
What she knows of the world,
Comes from prime-time television,
And her Mother.
Celina will die a virgin.
She masturbates rubbing astride the arm of the
 sofa,
She can't reach with her hands.

The Old House

I saw on the local news, just now, last night,
They're starting to take down the old house.
Too much damage from the second fire,
Started by vagrants, they say,
But I doubt it.
I always favour the unscrupulous, the less savoury.

The original home, they said,
Of some mayor or another,
Muttonchops, long dead.
Most recently a Greek house,
'Til taken by fire.

The pictures showed a toothy crane,
Bullying down the walls,
Slowly and bit by bit,
Cracking the windows,
Crunching the wood.
The pictures showed glimpses,
A mattress,
A bicycle,
A bath-tub with feet,
Hollyhock wallpaper,
Carpet scorched black.
The voice over was just words I could not hear.

The pictures showed its stately grounds,

Sloping to the river.
Overgrown now with alder and willow,
Black campfire marks,
Wine bottles and beer caps.
Kids I guess, from the neighbourhood.
Could be vagrants, I suppose,
But I doubt it,
It's not much of a town for vagrants,
More of a town for the unscrupulous, the less
    savoury.

The only time I touched the yellow brick,
It was just you and I,
It was just after the first fire.
It was wet, just finished raining,
It was autumn and cold and bleak.
You were thinking of buying,
I was moral support.

The only time I touched the yellow brick,
We gave that old house a good going over,
Climbed the stairs all careful,
Tipped up a couch and climbed it,
That we might peer in.
The air was rich with piss,
Redolent of rain and smoke.
The walls were scorched by flame.

The only time I touched the ghostly brick,
I climbed the porch all careful.

I skirted the holes and dangerous nails,
Reached back to the ground for you,
A tug, and easy does it,
A second to hold you steady.

The only time I touched the blackened brick,
Creepy cold and stolid,
My other hand was touching you.
You were soft,
But somehow stronger.
The voice over was just words I could not hear.

Make Lots

Did we get it, she asked?
Did we get every drop?
She covered me in beautiful torment.
I made some noise of heaven,
I made some noise of pain.
She bit my lip,
Her mouth was a fever,
Her mouth was a plum.
I made some sign of resurrection,
I made some sign of the cross.
Make more, she said.
Make lots and lots and lots.

SHAME

Charlie's dad's pet name for him was 'Fucken
   Retard'.
Charlie grew up knowing he never did anything
   right.
His mom gave him cake so he would stop crying.

Cindy was a heavy girl with thick glasses,
The kids at school called her 'Fatty Fatty Four-Eyes'
Cindy developed fast and early,
The boys would help themselves at recess,
Her mother gave her Valium so she would stop
   crying.

Pain is easy.
Pain is water.
Pain can be cried away.
Guilt is different.
Guilt is thick.
Guilt squeezes out like childbirth.
Shame is different.
Shame is thick.
Shame bleeds out like quicksilver.
Shame hits the ground and shatters.

I Am Martin Sheen

I wake.
I live.
I am Martin Sheen.

I have one room.
The note is there on the table.
I am a maudlin son of a bitch.
I am Martin Sheen.

I piss for an hour.
I piss sitting down.
I smell myself like poison.
I smell myself like cancer.
I start again.
I am Martin Sheen.

The note is there on the table.
I am a pathetic son of a bitch.
The pills are acid in me.
I am Martin Sheen.

I have a window.
I see bricks.
I see the side of a tree.
I hear truck sounds.
I am Martin Sheen.

I have a mirror.

I am Martin Sheen.

I hear the whump, whump, whump.
I am Martin Sheen.

The note is there on the table.
I am a sorry son of a bitch.
I am Martin Sheen.

I wake.
I live.
I am Martin Sheen.

The window has gone grey.
The window plays tree music.
The note is there on the table.
I am a poor excuse for a son of a bitch.
I am Martin Sheen.

I need smokes.
I need rye whiskey.
I need a can of food.
The note is there on the table.
I am a son of a bitch.
I am Martin Sheen.

I hear the whump, whump, whump.
The mirror has gone grey.
The window plays truck music.
The note is there on the table.
I am Martin Sheen.

Hopeless

Sleep well, she asked?
She was the type who asked if you slept well.
No, I said.
I knew with her it had to be the truth,
She sniffed out lies like truffles.

Bad dreams again, she asked?
She was the type who got to the heart of the
    matter.
Yes, I replied.
Want to talk it out, she asked?
She was the type who talked things out.
They're always the same, I said.
The same how, she asked?
She was the type who never settled,
She would probe, gentle, dangerous,
A dental tool in a careful hand.
Chaos, I said,
Hurried, frenetic, racing breathless around trying to
    make people understand,
Panic, I said,
Things going from worse to worse.
I can't make people understand,
They leave me hopeless, I said,
Hopeless and frustrated and scared,
Like things can never be right,

Can never be better because they were never any
 good,
Just always the same, or worse still, and worse still
 again.
Hmm, she said.
She was the type for whom 'Hmm' was a volume.

Was I part of your dream, she asked?
Was I one who wouldn't understand?
She pulled it from me like a stubborn cork.
Hmm, she said.

We drank coffee,
Listened to the television news.
Going to drink over it, she asked?
No, I replied, not today.
Hmm, she said.

We nibbled toast,
Stared at the television news.
Suicide, she asked?
No, I said, not today.
Hmm, she said.
She made it worse,
Made me feel hopeless,
Like some species of rescue thing.

Mascara

She pointed to a little pillow slip stain,
A scrawl, a hieroglyphic.
What's this, she asked?
She was foreign,
Her native language was one of those,
That, when spoken,
Sounded liked fighting,
Sounded on the verge of homicide and mayhem
    and violence.
In English, her voice was somber music.
I ignored her,
I busied myself with the window blinds.
What's this, she asked again, louder?
Just a stain, I said.
I busied myself with undressing.
She was naked, crouched on her knees,
Her back was long and tan,
I could already taste the clove taste of her.
She flicked at the black place with the tip of a
    reverent finger.
You were painting maybe, she asked?
I gave up.
It's mascara, all right, I said.
My voice was too loud,
My voice was beyond my control.
It's mascara and tears.
She stroked the black with the tip of a finger,

She stroked like she was reading from Braille.
Yours tears, she asked?
There was humour in her voice,
But none in her eyes,
They challenged.
I gave up.
No, not mine, I said.
I sat heavily on the bed.
From when, she asked?
From a long time ago?
I gave up.
Yes, I said, long enough.
She wiggled to face me.
I felt her hands, one soft on each shoulder.
Long enough, she said.
Her voice was soft,
Her voice was the long strings of a harp.

Grandpa

It is before first light in the morning in the
    summer.
I am at my grandparent's house.
My Grandpa is always the first one up,
I am always second,
I wake up when I hear him cough and spit.

My Grandpa gives me breakfast,
Thick bacon, thick bread, jam,
Coffee, treacly sweet and milky.

My Grandpa is always happy in the morning.
He jokes, he calls me monkey,
He calls me bat because I like the night time,
He jokes that he should hang me in the *buda*.
Buda is another word for closet,
Buda is a Polish word.

My Grandpa is always happy in the morning.
Outside, we piss against the fence.
Grandpa's house has no bathroom,
There is a shitter down a path.
I am afraid of the shitter,
It is dark and full of spiders.
The smell makes me cough.

My Grandpa is always happy in the morning.

Sometimes we work in the shop,
He sits me on the bench,
To watch him fix metal things.
His hands get very dirty,
He washes them in a pail of gas,
He dries them on his pants.

Sometimes we drive to town in his old red truck.
There is a hole in the floor, only one door works,
There is no glass in the back window.
My Grandpa calls the truck a son of a hoor.
I sit on my knees close beside him,
So that I can see out.
When we pass cows in a field,
He lets me push the silver lever for the horn.
My Grandpa is always happy in the morning.

In town, we visit at the gas station.
My Grandpa sits with the other men,
They roll cigarettes and smoke,
They drink from a bag.
My Grandpa shows me to the other men,
They rub my hair,
They call me my Polish name.
I wander around the lot and kick at things.

If we stay too long at the gas station,
My Mother will come to fetch me.
She yells at my Grandpa in angry Polish.
Grandpa laughs with the other men.

My Grandpa is always happy in the morning.

Sometimes at night, my Grandpa is angry.
He drinks black beer with my father,
With my uncles, with other men who smell like
    animals.
They drink lightning from glass jars in the
    basement,
They shout at each other.
Sometimes Grandpa will fight and break things,
Sometimes he will hit my Grandma and knock her
    down.
When it is scary and bad, I sleep under the piano
    bench,
Sometimes Grandpa sleeps on the floor near the
    furnace,
Or in the back of the truck.
My Grandpa is always happy in the morning.

When We Are Apart

When we are apart, I go off my feed.
When I try to sleep without my hand on your hip,
My heart acts up.
Sometimes, I feel like I have been breathless since
   the day we met.

First Kiss

We walked along in companionable silence,
We were friends but it was our first time,
Our first time alone together in the evening.
We were walking home from dinner,
Scallops and beef for me,
Salad and fish for her,
Ice cream parlour cones for dessert,
It was the first time I had seen her tongue,
Little and pink and lithe.

I had taken her hand when we crossed at the light,
And she had not thought to reclaim it.
Her hand in mine was dry and sweet like sugar,
I tried to do justice to her grasp.
The air brought me wisps of her scent,
We bumped occasionally, walking close,
She was small, barely to my shoulder.

I have a problem, she said.
(Let's assume she used my name,
And, further, that I cannot use it here.)
What's that, I asked?
(Let's assume I used her name,
And, further, that I cannot use it here.)
Is this a date, she asked?
I pondered this minefield for a long while.

We walked the sidewalk from circle to circle of
    light,
The evening was warm and middling moist.
Why do you ask, I bailed?
If it's a date, she said, won't you expect to kiss me
    good night?
I pondered this minefield for a long while.

We walked the sidewalk from circle to circle of
    light,
We allowed a dog-walker to pass us by,
Carrying a plastic bag lumpy with shit.
I wouldn't expect a kiss good night, I said,
But I would like one very much.
I'd like to think however, that when it comes to
    good night,
We would kiss each other so,
The way you phrased it made it sound quite one-
    sided.
Fair enough, she said.
We walked along in companionable silence.

So, if this is a date, she said, or something quite
    like it,
And we are expecting to kiss each other good
    night,
Well, I have a problem with that.
I pondered this minefield for a long while.

We walked the sidewalk from circle to circle of
    light,
We stopped at a corner and waited for a turning
    car.
What problem is that, I bailed?
What if we kiss just awful, she asked?
What if we knock teeth or get sloppy?
What if you go left and I go right,
And we can't find the centre?
I pondered this minefield for a long while.

The street had run out of light,
We were in near full darkness, houses to our left,
A sudden ghost of a children's park to our right.
I have an idea, I said.
I knew you would, she said.
I felt the strength of her smile without looking.
She gave my hand a clench.
What if we had a trial kiss, I asked?
Just up there where the light rebegins,
We'll stop under the light so that we can see,
We'll try a short kiss to see if it's awful,
To see if we find the centre.
Okay, she said.
We walked along in companionable silence.

There, where the light rebegan,
We turned toward each other and met in the
    middle.

She looked up at me through long and auburn
    lashes,
Her lips were glisteny moist as if she had just
    licked them,
I wondered briefly at the state of mine.
I grasped her at the points of her shoulders,
Cupping her there in my palms.
(I thought briefly of my parent holding me there.
Heard, I'll shake some sense into you,
Pushed it from my mind.)
She raised her hands to my waist,
And held me there bird wing gentle.
We came together at the mouth,
Just a touch at first, for the feel,
Pulled back,
Reseated for comfort and breadth.
Turning together we found our centre,
Pulled away, back for a bit and finally away,
Her lower lip sucked slightly between mine,
My upper lip sucked slightly between hers.
We leaned apart.
She looked up at me through long and auburn
    lashes,
Raised one hand from my waist to my neck,
Just there toward the back,
Pulled me in again, nails digging in slightly,
Pushing up goose flesh,
Her thumb hard on some artery under my ear,
I felt somewhat faint, dizzy,
The center found us right off,

Deeper, more profound,
It was the first time I had tasted her tongue,
Little and moist and lithe.
She looked up at me through long and auburn
   lashes,
I think we'll do just fine, I said.
Yah, we're good, she said.

We turned and started away,
We walked the sidewalk from circle to circle of
   light,
We neared her little cottage house.
I apologize, I said.
What for, she asked?
I kissed a little roughly there, the second time, I
   said,
It was like I was suddenly hungry for your mouth.
She gave my hand a clench.
I understand, she said.

We walked along in companionable silence.
The air brought me wisps of her scent,
We bumped occasionally, walking close,
She was small, barely to my shoulder.

NANCY

We lay in fever's glide path,
Drying slowly in the soft air from the balcony door.
She said to me;
"Do you know why I cry sometimes when we're
   having sex?"
I, who had several theories,
But none I wished to voice,
For the sex was somewhat good and plentiful,
She was skilled with her mouth,
She always had money and a car,
I fancied myself in love,
Could say only "No, why?",
In an off-hand, tired sort of way.
"Sometimes when I'm having an orgasm," she said,
"I think that I'm going to die.
It feels like you're killing me with your cock."
I, in response, the best that I could summon,
Me, the Bonaparte of the *bon mot*,
The *paramour* of the *beau geste*,
The best that I could summon in response was,
"Is that right."
There was some silence.
She was a master of silence,
She had learned it at her mother's knee.
"It's just a thing," she said.
"I've learned to live with it.
I think it has something to do with my father."

I, in response, the best that I could summon,
Me, the master of wry wit,
The Algonquin Round Table of my peers,
The best that I could summon in response was,
A simple, long delayed,
"Hmmm".
"My father hates you," she said,
Apropos of nothing at all.
"He says he wouldn't touch you with a ten-foot
    pole."
To that I could not respond at all,
I knew it to be true.
He had hissed it to me *soto voce*,
The last time I had been to dinner.
Hopped up on mushrooms,
Stoned on gin,
I hadn't given a good goddamn.
To that I did not respond at all.
Eventually she rolled away from me,
My skin turned wetly cold,
Just where we had been touching.

Game Over

Before,
Before there was this,
It was late innings.

Before,
Before there was this,
There was only you.

Before,
Before there was this,
There were eyes from under lashes,
There was chestnut hair,
There was the skin at the top of your back,
There, just there,
There, where it becomes your neck.

Before,
Before there was this,
There were the teeth of your smile,
There was the touch of your hand.
Before,
Before there was this,
There was the smell of you,
My goodness.

Now,
Now there is this.

I have tasted of you,
And my food is so much sand.
I have drunk of you,
And my thirst cannot be quenched.
My heart, my cheeks, my lips,
They burn.

Now,
Now there is this.
I am desperate,
Unfocused.
I have lost my memory,
I have lost my mind.

Before,
Before there was this,
It was late innings.

Now,
Now that I've kissed you once,
It's game over.

THE ORGAN

When we were small,
My sisters and I,
We would play the organ,
At the end of the hall,
Of our Grandma's house.
Ill-supervised, we played perhaps rough,
By mid-morning my grandmother,
Was usually lost in drink.

To us the organ was a fantasy.
Dark wood, almost black.
Tall as a house it seemed,
Ornately carved curlicues,
Feathered with dust.
We had been abandoned by our parents,
Our parents were lost in drink,

The organ had a round stool.
Of leather and horsehair.
It had a corkscrew base.
We would spin,
Until we dropped to the floor,
Vertiginous,
As if we were lost in drink.

We played music of a sort.
Two of us on the floor,

To pump the squeaking pedals,
Two of us at the keys,
Yellow ivory and faded black.
We played music,
Discordant and raucous and harsh.

Of late, I hear that selfsame music,
Discordant and raucous and harsh.
It seems to come,
From within the walls of my bedroom.
It reverberates,
It shimmies the paint.
It makes me smile to hear it,
I am lost in drink.

He Has Lost Control Of The Angels

I know with all my heart,
That the last ice age,
Was the act of an insane God,
That in freezing the earth,
He sought to honour the cougars,
By turning them to fleet rivers unflowing,
To make love to the deer,
By making of them birch trees,
Unmoving, yet swift.

All this I heard from his own lips,
In one of his more lucid moments.
He speaks slowly and clearly,
In a language I think German,
When he speaks at all.

We used to play bridge together,
Until, some time ago,
He collapsed at table,
Weeping and moaning for the cougars.
We sent for his wife,
Who gathered him up and led him home,
Billing and cooing and stroking his hands.

Since then he just stands in the surf,
He gazes out to sea.
His wife no longer allows him to ride.
He has lost control of the angels.

Here Is How It Is

Here is how it is these days.
Here is how I am.
I sleep often.
I rise early.
I nap in the afternoon from disinterest.
My sleep is troubled,
My dreams broken, jagged.
I wake in a sweat,
Hands beneath the pillow,
Cramped from grasping.
I am in love,
But that love brings me no joy.

I think in secret.
I drink in secret.
Vodka, past the heart, straight to the brain,
That's my drink of choice.
I am short-tempered,
Miserable,
Argumentative at home.
In public, I am better,
I make a show of being cheerful,
Human.
I have no appetite for food,
I have a thirst that cannot be quenched.
I am in love,
But that love brings me no joy.

I find solace in books I have read before,
I read nothing new.
I do nothing constructive.
I cannot abide video.
I cannot sit still.
I write poems to destroy them,
Abortions of words,
Genocide.
I am in love,
But that love brings me no joy.

I have not looked my wife in the eye forever.
I kiss her neck,
But my lips are miles distant.
She senses something amiss.
She seeks to hold me to her.
I have told so many lies,
The truth is miles deep.
I kiss her neck.
I hold her to me,
With arms miles distant.
I am in love,
But that love brings me no joy.

I contemplate my death.
I plan it.
I consider the deaths of others,
Admire them,
Revile them.

I search for courage,
Research resolve.
My family is a cipher,
My friends, a memory.
I am in danger of going blind.
I am in love,
But that love brings me no joy.

I see her on the street a million times,
Chestnut hair flowing.
I reach for her.
I reach for the phone.
I reach for my vodka,
Straight, past the heart, to the brain.
I live my life by the rules of another,
I have no life at all.
I broke a rule.
I reap the whirlwind.
I plough the sea.
I am in love,
But that love brings me no joy.

I live vicarious.
I have no original thought.
I respond to stimuli,
I react.
Dog-walkers make me cry.
I hate the colour orange.
I have vague memories of smiles,
But my face forgets.
I am in love,

But that love brings me no joy.

Guilt is my constant companion,
Guilt is my seeing eye dog.
I have the diamond guilt of the Jew.
I have the charisma of the camp commandant.
I have the swagger of the new oven guard,
Proud and shamed,
Head up, eyes down.
People shy away from me,
They make excuses,
They smell guilt on me like offal.
They turn their heads,
Press sleeves to nose.
They leave me to myself.
Alone, I feel unsafe,
Weary, uncertain,
Nowhere near stable.
I cannot be left to my own devices.
My mind is elsewhere,
I fear its return.
I am in love,
But that love brings me no joy.

Just Then, Just There

Just then,
I caught my glimpse of heaven,
Just there, where your shoulder becomes your
 neck.
In that capillary web,
Gossamer blue,
I unraveled a mystery,
And I fell.

Hearsay

Here is a thing that happened to a good friend of
 mine,
It was told to me in a drunken haze,
This I know to be true,
Or very nearly so.

I imagine he showed evidence at some point,
I must have seen it in black and white through an
 alcoholic glare,
This I know to be true,
Or very nearly so.

I write it down in free form verse for that is how I
 think these days,
I think I think in free form verse,
I know I lie almost all the time,
Sometimes, I lie in free form verse,
Sometimes, I think in lies.

Here's what my friend told me,
So far as I can remember.
I might have added to the facts, perhaps taken
 away,
I might have polished the prose, added
 punctuation, a literary tilt or two,
Edited for space or content.
I might have made it up wholesale.

I might have imagined the whole thing.
I might have imagined the friend or the woman or
    both.
I might have imagined it all in free form verse.
I might have simply wished it would happen.
It was late.
It was dark.
Who can remember things for sure?

Good story though, its provenance
    notwithstanding,
True story.
Here it is in his own words,
Or what his words would be,
If he had spoken and I'm very nearly sure he did.
I know I hear voices,
They speak the truth to me in free form verse.
This I know to be true.
Or very nearly so.

Then again perhaps the voices lie in free form
    verse,
Perhaps they speak not at all.
All things considered,
I think I cannot be trusted,
This I know to be true,
Or very nearly so.

Here is the best exchange I ever had,
The best exchange of any kind.

It happened when I was busy,
Falling in love with a stubborn, magical woman,
The woman that you wait for,
The woman you doubt will ever appear,
Until she appears and you are caught unprepared,
Best shirt crumpled near the bed,
Two best pants at the cleaners,
Hair two weeks past a cut,
Unshaven.
Her, some hidden wind machine,
Softly blowing her hair,
Some scent, cinnamon or magnolia.
You can see your face in her bottom lip.

She wrote to me....

"Do you remember when we walked to my car in the parking garage?"

I wrote back....

"Of course.
You took my hand and asked, is this alright?
And I answered,
Completely.
Perfect."

(What I did not write was....
Your hand was marble, cool and chill.
It pulsed.
I held it careful,

A glass hand grenade,
Pin out,
Careful.)

She wrote to me....

"Do you remember our first kiss?
We leaned up against my car.
I got dust on my pants."

I wrote back....

"Of course."

(The taste of your lipstick had become my favourite
    thing.)

She wrote to me....

"I think that is the best kiss I ever had in my life.
I will never not feel you on my lips."

I wrote back....

"Likewise."

She wrote to me....

"Do you remember our second kiss,
After we caught our breath,
When we switched positions?
I placed my palms on your stubbly cheeks,

I pulled your face to mine."

I wrote back....

"Who could forget such a thing?
I got dust on my pants."

(Your palms were cool like marble,
Your lips warm like silver,
Strong and thin like Caribbean dogs,
My cheeks will never be the same.)

She wrote to me....

"I think that is the best kiss I ever had in my life.
Your tongue was sweet-flavoured and gentle,
I wanted to eat you."

I wrote back....

"Likewise."

She wrote to me....

"Do you remember the third kiss of our life,
The one where you leaned in my car window?
You kissed me rough,
Hungry,
Almost violent.
You bit my lip."

I wrote back....

"I apologize.
I got carried away."

(I still feel the press of the window's frame,
Across my neck.
Your teeth as they clattered on mine.
The weight of your tongue.)

She wrote to me....

"I think that is the best kiss I ever had in my life.
I liked that you just took it,
Like it had always belonged to you."

I wrote back....

"Likewise."

She wrote to me....

"Do you remember the last kiss we shared,
The one you kissed into my palm through the open
    window,
The one that lingered,
The one you said was my traveler?"

I wrote back....

"Absolutely."

(For I spit a part of my heart into your palm with
　　that kiss,
Trusting you with its safe-keeping.)

She wrote to me....

"I think that is the best kiss I ever had in my life.
My palm hummed as with stigmata."

She wrote to me....

"I kissed that kiss before you were out of sight.
I licked my palm,
That I might taste you again.
Now I'm fresh out.
Might I have another or a few?"

I ran to her,
In my third best pants.
She was that kind of woman,
The kind that you run to,
For the rest of your life.

The Gap

Will you do something for me, I ask?

We are home from being out.
It is night, late.
We are in our bedroom.
I am sitting on the end of the bed.
You are at the window.
You are adjusting the blind,
You are forever adjusting that blind.

Of course, you say.

Will you undress for me, I ask?

Your face becomes amused.
Your voice becomes laughter.

Like a strip tease, you ask?

Not at all, I say,
Just undress,
Undress like a beautiful woman would undress,
If she were alone,
Just here, in front of the bed, in the centre of the
    room.

Your eyes search me.

Your eyes go serious deep.

Why, you ask? Why tonight?

Just because, I say,
Because I love you,
Because you are the most beautiful woman in the
    world,
Because I want to love you with my eyes.

Your eyes search me.
Your eyes go serious deep.
You smile.
You do that thing with your eyes and your
    forehead,
That thing that wrecks my heart.
You smile.

Okay, you say,
But I think you're a fool.

You smile.
You stoop and work the straps of your shoes,
Shoes careful in the closet with their friends.
Now jewelry, now a shake of the hair,
It blossoms like fire and I lose my mind.

You unbutton your blouse,
Pull it from your skirt,
Loose and off and into the hamper.

Your skin has taken on a flush.

You work a secret skirt button off to the side,
You step out,
Loose and off and careful on a hanger.

You stand in lingerie.
Your skin has taken on a flush.
Your eyes search me.
Your eyes go serious deep.
I lose my mind.
I smile.

Arms behind in that twisty woman way,
You loose your breasts.
You toss the bra at me,
I catch it and lay it beside me on the bed.
A slither for the slip,
A wiggle and you are bare.

You stand, little girl nervous,
Hands clasped in front.
I reach for you.

Come closer, I say.

You smile.
I thought you were going to love me with your
    eyes, you say.
I misspoke, I say.

I lied.
I changed my mind.
I neglected to mention,
I want to love you with the tips of my fingers.

You smile.
You close the gap.

You stand, little girl nervous,
Hands clasped in front.
I put the tips of my fingers on you,
High on your shoulders,
I ride them down to hands clasped in front.
I take one hand,
I kiss the tip of each finger,
I push that hand to the side.
I take one hand,
I kiss the tip of each finger,
I push that hand to the side.
Your eyes are closed.
Your skin has taken on a flush.
Your skin is fresh and chill.

I put the tips of my fingers high on your chest,
I ride them down the slopes of you.
The muscles of your stomach ripple and clench.
I smile.
I lose my mind.

I turn you slowly.

I put the tips of my fingers high on your back,
I ride them down the smooth of you.

I turn you gently.
I kiss a nipple,
I kiss a nipple.
You skin has taken on a flush.
Your skin is fresh and chill.

That wasn't your eyes, you say.
That wasn't the tips of your fingers.
I misspoke, I say.
I lied.
I changed my mind.
I neglected to mention,
I want to love you with my lips.
I want to love you with the flat of my tongue.

You smile.
You do that thing with your eyes and your
   forehead,
That thing that wrecks me.
You close the gap.

LITTLE SPOON

Are you asleep – she asked from behind me?
No – I said.
I was, but I had a dream and the dream woke me up.
I thought our loving would have knocked you out – she said.
I know it did me.
I sleep like a baby in your bed.
I don't think I ever slept like a baby – I said – even when I was a baby.
You were a beautiful baby – she said.
I've seen the pictures.
You were cute as a bug's ear.
I wanted to eat you up.
I felt her teeth high on my back.
I shuddered, repulsed.

Was it a good dream – she asked from behind me?
No – I said, it was bad.
I was at some event, a reunion, a celebration in my hometown.
I was drinking again, but I was okay,
I was drinking Molson Export from the bottle and playing darts.
It was okay for a while then things got bad,
I was searching for something I could not find,

Searching and searching for someone I could not
 find,
There were tents and tunnels and I was lost,
There were fences and walls and darkness and I
 was lost.
Everything was covered with tarpaulin.
There were people that I needed but they were
 always somewhere else,
I was lost.
There was a woman too and she was very cruel.
If I had been there – she said – I would have
 punched her and kicked her and pulled her hair.
No – I said – I was crueler to her.
I was cruel to her first.
I felt her hand on my hip.
I shuddered, repulsed.

Andre was in the dream too – I said.
He was drunk and happy and carefree.
He was whistling.
Do I know him – she asked?
No – I said – he is a friend from another life a long
 time ago.
He is still out there.
He has fallen over the edge.
In the dream, I was chasing him, warning him, but
 he did not listen,
Maybe he could not hear, maybe I was mute.
He went into a place where I knew he would die.

I couldn't follow because I would die too and I was
    never that brave.
I think you're quite brave – she said.
I know where you've been.
She kissed the blade of my shoulder.
I shuddered, repulsed.

I wish you were like me – she said.
I never dream.
My brain just turns off,
Like Steinbeck said, you know, like shutting a
    closet door.
My brain is not like that – I said.
My brain is all wires and on the wires are birds,
Ravens or cowbirds or tiny crow birds with beaks
    like black pins.
They fly and they land and they set off a terrible
    vibration.
They are never at rest.
They leave sometimes but they always come back.
They have evil eyes, black as fountain pen ink.
They look at me with hate or scorn or anger,
I can see them shrieking but I cannot hear.
Maybe they are mute.
Sometimes a wire breaks.
She hunched in closer.
I shuddered, repulsed.

You used to sleep all wrapped around me – she
    said,

You used to surround me.
I felt so safe when you used to surround me and I
   was the little spoon.
I remember – I said.
You were scared and I loved you.
I surrounded you so you would feel safe.
Now you're scared – she said.
You're scared and I love you.
Now you can be the little spoon,
I will be the big spoon and I will surround you and
   you will feel safe.
She hunched closer.
She wrapped all around me.
She sang some nonsense song soft in my ear,
She whispered and the birds fell to sleep.
She whispered and sang some nonsense song and
   shut the closet door.

Blue In The Face

You're not much for emotion, are you – she asked?
We were quiet, quiescent, finished with love.
It was raining, the room damp and warm,
The room was a wallpaper womb.
Not really – I said.
I only have two, anger and fear.
What are you mad at – she asked?
Everything – I said.
Hmm – she said in her special way,
That made me want to murder her or love her for
  the rest of my life.
What are you afraid of – she asked?
Everything – I said.
Hmm – she said in her special way,
That made me want to cover her with kisses or
  chop off her head.
Maybe you should talk to someone about that –
  she said.
I have – I said.
I've talked 'til I'm blue in the face.
She looked me close.
She looked my face like she was looking for blue.
Hmm – she said in her special way,
That made me want to punch her or marry her in a
  church.
Talking doesn't work for me – I said,
I'm not able to tell the truth.

Hmm – she said in her special way,
That made me want to hear her cry or scream with joy.
Maybe you should talk to someone about that – she said.
I have – I said.
I've talked 'til I'm blue in the face.
Hmm – she said in her special way,
That made me want to strangle her or stroke the hair near her ears.
She let it go and fell to sleep.
I rolled up and put my feet on the floor.
I rolled up and put my face in my hands.
It was raining, the room damp and warm,
The room was a wallpaper womb.
The room was a circle.
The day was a trap.

LIFE IS SCHOOL

Before, at the bottom, in the pit,
I learned that I smell like my grandfather.
I smell like the inside of my grandfather's hat.
I stink like pork and ammonia.
I reek of liquor and sweat.

In the middle, in the ambulance bed,
All tied up,
All tied down,
Driving fast on a rain-slick road,
Driving noisy in the early of the night,
I studied my hands.
I have my father's hands,
Reptile hands, yellow like parchment,
Wretched hands, old like an Egyptian king.

After, at the window,
Looking down at the jaws of the street,
Reaching up to eat me,
I came to know that a woman waiting at a bus-stop,
Is the most beautiful thing in the world.
I learned that a woman waiting at a bus-stop,
Holding a small and shiny, hard-shelled purse,
Clutched close to her chest,
Is the most dangerous thing in the world.

Life is school.
I have been left back.

Poet and novelist Michael Kuiack was first published at the age of 12. More recently, he was the winner of the Poetry London Annual Poetry Contest in 2012 (Miracle On South Street) and 2014 (Life Is School), both of which poems are included in this volume. A long-time resident of Ontario, he now lives in Kelowna, British Columbia. *Here There Be Tygers* is his first poetry collection.

www.ingramcontent.com/pod-product-compliance
Lightning Source LLC
Chambersburg PA
CBHW071455070426
42452CB00040B/1531